ALEX GIBSON

763·11
GB

NEOLITHIC AND EARLY
BRONZE AGE POTTERY

GW00568208

GY

042189

2

Cover photograph
A food vessel urn from Ryton, Tyne and Wear
(drawn in figure **16, 3**).
(Museum of Antiquities of the University and Society of Antiquaries,
Newcastle upon Tyne.)

British Library Cataloguing in Publication Data available

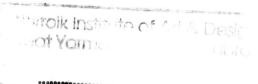
Published by
SHIRE PUBLICATIONS LTD
Cromwell House, Church Street, Princes Risborough,
Aylesbury, Bucks HP17 9AJ, UK.

Series Editor: James Dyer

ISBN 0 85263 755 1

First published 1986

Set in 11 point Times and printed in Great Britain by
C. I. Thomas & Sons (Haverfordwest) Ltd,
Press Buildings, Merlins Bridge, Haverfordwest, Dyfed

Contents

4

List of illustrations

Chronological chart *page 6*
Fig. 1. Terms used in pottery descriptions *page 9*
Fig. 2. Grimston ware *page 12*
Fig. 3. Hembury ware *page 14*
Fig. 4. Windmill Hill pottery *page 15*
Fig. 5. Abingdon and Mildenhall pottery *page 16*
Fig. 6. Whitehawk pottery *page 17*
Fig. 7. Peterborough ware *page 20*
Fig. 8. Northern impressed pottery *page 22*
Fig. 9. Grooved ware *page 25*
Fig. 10. Scottish regional neolithic bowls *page 29*
Fig. 11. Beaker pottery *page 32*
Fig. 12. Vase food vessels *page 37*
Fig. 13. Vase food vessels *page 37*
Fig. 14. Bowl food vessels *page 38*
Fig. 15. Enlarged food vessels *page 39*
Fig. 16. Enlarged food vessels *page 40*
Fig. 17. Collared urns *page 43*
Fig. 18. Pygmy cups *page 45*
Fig. 19. Regional bronze age pottery *page 47*
Fig. 20. Biconical and cordoned urns *page 48*
Fig. 21. Deverel-Rimbury pottery *page 51*
Fig. 22. Regional bronze age urn forms *page 52*

Plate 1. Early neolithic pottery from south-west England *page 13*
Plate 2. Beaker pottery *page 33*
Plate 3. Food vessels *page 36*
Plate 4. Encrusted urns *page 41*
Plate 5. Decorative techniques *page 55*

Preface and acknowledgements

The pottery of the neolithic, or late stone age, and the early bronze age is a large subject. There is a large variety not only of national types but also of regional styles and sub-styles. This book is intended as a guide to these styles from Britain during the period from 4000 to 1000 bc. No attempt has been made to discuss the material from Ireland as there is as great a variety of pottery there and a similar book could be devoted to that country alone. It is hoped that this will serve as an outline to the main types of pottery found in the excavation of neolithic and bronze age sites and an attempt has been made to describe each of these styles in enough detail to give the reader a general understanding of the pottery.

It is not necessary to read this book from cover to cover. It should be treated as a guide to be dipped into at the relevant sections. Readers new to the subject should perhaps read the introduction and consult the glossary first. In the main, however, pottery description is simple and logical. Collared urns are just that, urns with collars.

I would like to thank all the people who have offered advice and help during the preparation of this book and in particular Professor D. D. A. Simpson who has helped from an early stage and who commented on the typescript. Dr H. A. W. Burl has also commented on the typescript and to both gentlemen I offer my thanks and appreciation for their time and candour. Miss R. J. Cresswell has helped with the typescript and the illustrations, and I would also like to thank two of my colleagues from Leicester University's Department of Archaeology, Mr F. M. B. Cooke for photographic work and Miss A. J. Woods for commenting on the glossary.

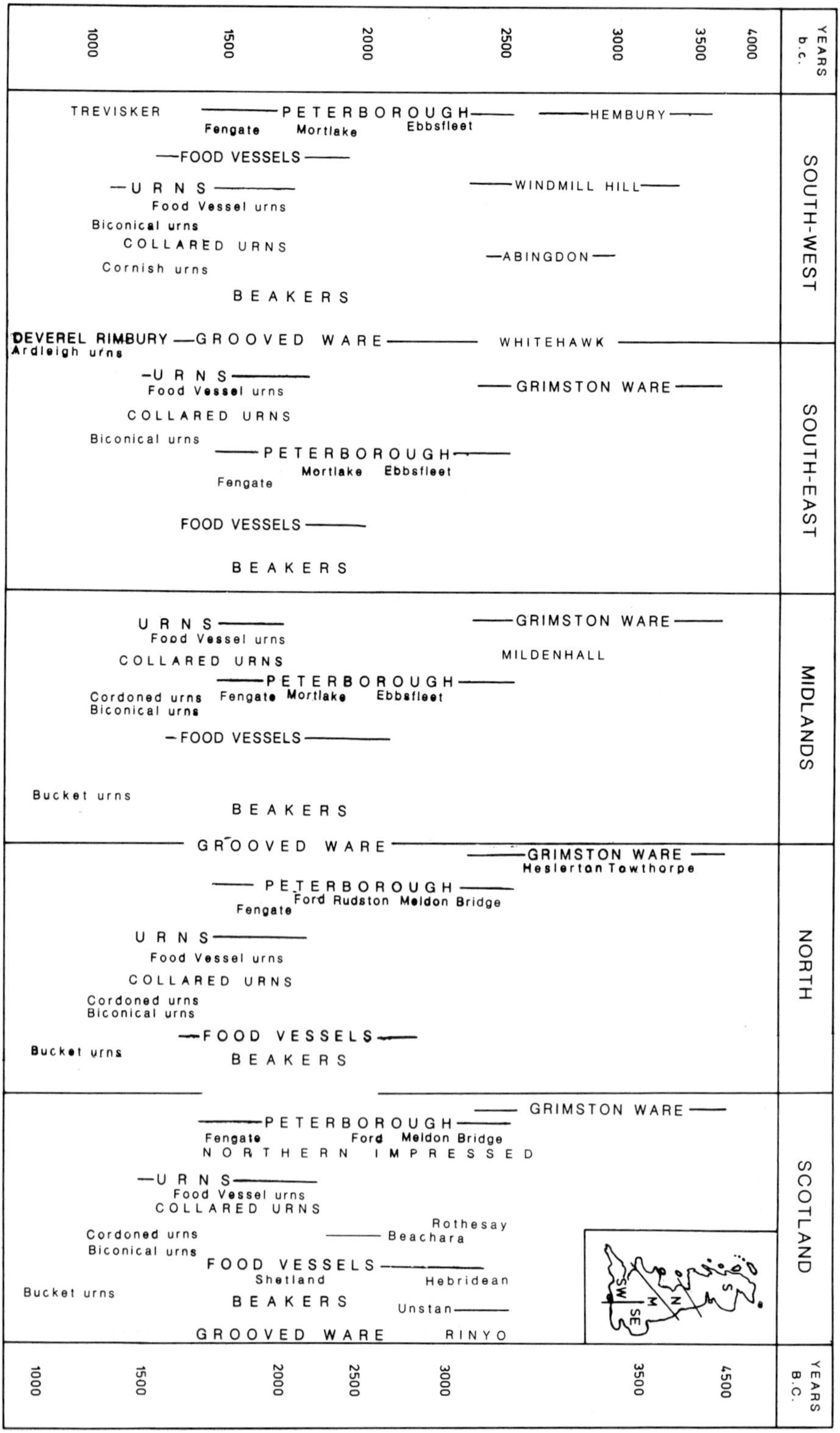

YEARS b.c.	1000	1500	2000	2500	3000	3500	4000	

SOUTH-WEST

TREVISKER ——— P E T E R B O R O U G H ——— ——— HEMBURY ———
Fengate   Mortlake   Ebbsfleet
—FOOD VESSELS ———
—U R N S ———   ——— WINDMILL HILL ———
Food Vessel urns
Biconical urns
COLLARED URNS
Cornish urns   —ABINGDON—
B E A K E R S

SOUTH-EAST

DEVEREL RIMBURY —GROOVED WARE ———   WHITEHAWK ———
Ardleigh urns
—U R N S ———   ——— GRIMSTON WARE ———
Food Vessel urns
COLLARED URNS
Biconical urns   — P E T E R B O R O U G H ——
Fengate   Mortlake   Ebbsfleet
FOOD VESSELS ———
B E A K E R S

MIDLANDS

U R N S ———   ——— GRIMSTON WARE ———
Food Vessel urns
COLLARED URNS   MILDENHALL
— P E T E R B O R O U G H ——
Cordoned urns Fengate Mortlake Ebbsfleet
Biconical urns
— FOOD VESSELS ———
Bucket urns
B E A K E R S

NORTH

——— G R O O V E D   W A R E ———   ——— GRIMSTON WARE ———
Heslerton Towthorpe
——— P E T E R B O R O U G H ——
Fengate   Ford Rudston Meldon Bridge
U R N S ———
Food Vessel urns
COLLARED URNS
Cordoned urns
Biconical urns
—FOOD VESSELS ———
Bucket urns
B E A K E R S

SCOTLAND

——— GRIMSTON WARE ———
— P E T E R B O R O U G H ——
Fengate   Ford Meldon Bridge
N O R T H E R N   I M P R E S S E D
—U R N S ———
Food Vessel urns
COLLARED URNS   Rothesay
Cordoned urns   ——— Beachara
Biconical urns
FOOD VESSELS ———
Shetland   Hebridean
Bucket urns
B E A K E R S   Unstan———
G R O O V E D   W A R E   RINYO

YEARS B.C.	1000	1500	2000	2500	3000		3500	4500

1
Introduction

It is the durability of pottery that has made it so important to archaeologists. Pottery was made in Britain from the time of the first farmers in the early fourth millennium bc and was used for religious and domestic purposes. Some vessels were later deposited in a ritual act or discarded when broken and thus entered the archaeological record. The survival potential of fired clay is remarkable, and in the excavation of neolithic and bronze age sites broken pieces of pottery, or *sherds,* may be found in large numbers, and many may be reconstructable.

Because pottery changes in shape and decoration over time, sherds constitute one of the main dating tools of the archaeologist, and it is for this reason that pottery is so important and has been studied so frequently. Pottery studies, however, have not only been concerned with the shape and decoration of the vessels but have also included the analysis of clays and their inclusions, which allows the identification of local styles and areas of manufacture. This is not to suggest that all the problems relating to prehistoric pottery have been solved, however, and many new problems arise from each new study and from the development of new archaeological techniques. For example, radiocarbon dating has shown that the old established chronologies are either no longer valid or are relevant to distinct geographical areas rather than nationally.

The change from the stone age to the bronze age was a gradual development that lasted many centuries and consequently there is a great overlap in the pottery from the periods. Some late neolithic styles, for example Peterborough ware, co-existed at least partly with early bronze age forms such as food vessels. This can clearly be seen on the chronological chart opposite. The changes in pottery styles must be seen as a series of gradual mergers rather than fixed point breaks.

Radiocarbon dating

The discovery of this technique was revolutionary because for the first time archaeologists had a means of discovering how old prehistoric artefacts actually were, whereas previously they had relied on relative chronologies based on artefact development and calculated guesswork.

The technique assesses the amount of radioactive carbon 14,

found in all living organisms, remaining in organic material. The rate of decay of carbon 14 is known and by measuring the degree of radioactivity present in an archaeological sample the date of that sample can be determined. The date obtained, however, is never exact and will always be expressed with a margin of error such as '1500± 100 bc'. This date means that there is a 60 per cent chance that the actual date will lie between 1600 and 1400 bc. A radiocarbon date is always expressed as bc or ad to distinguish it from a true calendar date which is BC or AD. The reason for this is that it is now known that radiocarbon dates do not equate with calendar dates because the carbon 14 has been affected by fluctuations in background atmospheric radiation levels. To achieve a calendar date it is necessary to recalibrate the radiocarbon date. Some archaeologists prefer not to do this but to deal only with radiocarbon years, in bc or ad. In this book all the dates given are carbon 14 dates and are expressed as bc. A recalibrated chronology is given as years BC in the chronological chart.

Technology of pottery

Pottery, or ceramic, consists of clay that has been chemically changed and hardened using heat to drive out the water present in the molecules. If the clay has been properly fired, it will hold water and will not soften. If imperfectly fired, however, the clay will revert back to its liquid state on contact with water or anything wet. Clay sources of varying quality are found commonly in Britain and whereas a coarse clay may need to be fined before use a very fine clay may need to have coarse materials added.

In specialist pottery descriptions in archaeological excavation reports reference is frequently made to *inclusions*. These are non-clay bodies found in the fabric of the pottery and are either naturally occurring or added. The former group may be small sand grains, quartz or organic remains, for example, which occur naturally in the clay itself and are derived from the local geology or ecology. The latter have been deliberately added to the clay to reduce the plasticity and to open the fabric so that during the firing process water can easily escape and will not blow out rapidly and cause the pot to explode. Almost any material is suitable for this and small pieces of crushed pottery (grog), sand, grass, crushed flint and shell are all commonly found in prehistoric pottery.

Once the clay had been prepared and the pot fashioned,

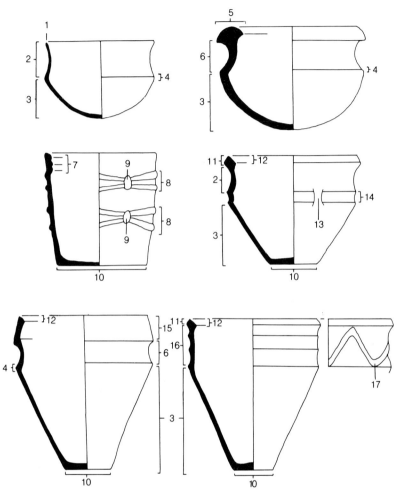

Fig. 1. A guide to the terms used in pottery descriptions. 1, rim; 2, neck; 3, belly; 4, carination or shoulder; 5, rim moulding; 6, neck or cavetto zone; 7, internal rim mouldings; 8, raised or applied cordons; 9, raised or applied lugs; 10, base; 11, external rim moulding; 12, internal rim bevel; 13, shoulder lug or stop; 14, shoulder cavetto zone; 15, collar; 16, multiple cavetto zones numbered consecutively from the top; 17, applied chevrons.

usually from a series of coils as the potter's wheel was unknown in Britain at this time, the vessels could be burnished or decorated in a variety of ways. Impressed techniques, where a material such as string or bone was pushed into the damp clay, are very common in the neolithic and bronze age as are incised decoration and applied or raised cordons and lugs. Once the pot has dried, it is then ready for firing. Like the potter's wheel, kilns are unknown in the British neolithic and bronze age so the pottery would have to be fired in a bonfire. The absence of archaeological evidence for manufacturing sites suggests that potting was perhaps a domestic chore with one or two vessels being fired at a time in a small fire. This, however, may be reading too much into the gap in the archaeological record and it may simply be that firing sites lay away from the main settlement to prevent a fire hazard and have consequently not been discovered.

Terminology

Figure **1** offers a simple guide to the most commonly used terms in pottery descriptions and to the most frequently found vessel forms in the neolithic and bronze age. Most of these terms are self-explanatory and straightforward but others, such as *carination* and *cavetto zone,* are rather more specific and would not necessarily be found outside pottery studies. Though there is no formalised or accepted convention for the terminology of pot forms and features, those named in figure **1** and in the glossary will be met with frequently in archaeological literature and pottery reports. The illustrated vessels are referred to in the text by the figure and drawing number thus (**1,** 6).

2
The early neolithic

Pottery first reached the British Isles with the first neolithic farmers in the fourth millennium bc. This was probably a result of the introduction of a more settled way of life that is associated with farming in contrast to the nomadic habit of the mesolithic hunter-gatherers: the fragility of pottery does not lend itself to constant movement across a land without roads and wheeled transport.

The earliest pots seem to be the simple and undecorated pots, cups and bowls which were originally labelled Windmill Hill ware by Piggott in 1931 but which have subsequently been divided into regional forms.

The earliest dated pottery in Britain is *Grimston-Lyles Hill* ware and it is also one of the longest lasting styles, probably as a result of its simplicity (**2**). Carbon 14 dates suggest that this style started around 3500 bc and may have remained in use for well over a millennium. The tradition is also distributed widely over Great Britain from Caithness to East Anglia and is part of a wider western European tradition. The major characteristic of the series is the stylistic conservatism and the comparatively few vessel forms. The pottery is almost invariably undecorated, exceptions to the rule being vessels with slight fluting, and the majority of the vessels are either carinated or 'S'-profiled round-based bowls (**2**, 1, 2, 3). Simple hemispherical cups or bowls are also found in the assemblage (**2**, 5). The rim forms are rarely elaborate and are usually either thickened, simple (**2**, 1), or rolled (**2**, 3). Applied lugs may be found on the carinations of bowls or the exteriors of cups, but they are rare. The fabric of Grimston ware is usually good and fine and frequently burnished but occasionally inclusions will either have burnt or dissolved out of the surfaces to give a 'corky' texture (**2**, 1).

It comes as no surprise that regional variations are frequently found in a series as geographically widespread as Grimston ware. There are, for example, three sub-styles in Yorkshire — Grimston ware itself (**2**, 3), *Heslerton ware* (**2**, 4), and *Towthorpe* bowls (**2**, 5). Heslerton ware differs from Grimston ware in that the 'S' profile is slacker with no sharp carination and with a rather more open appearance. Towthorpe ware is characterised by open hemispherical bowls with out-turned rims and occasionally applied lugs.

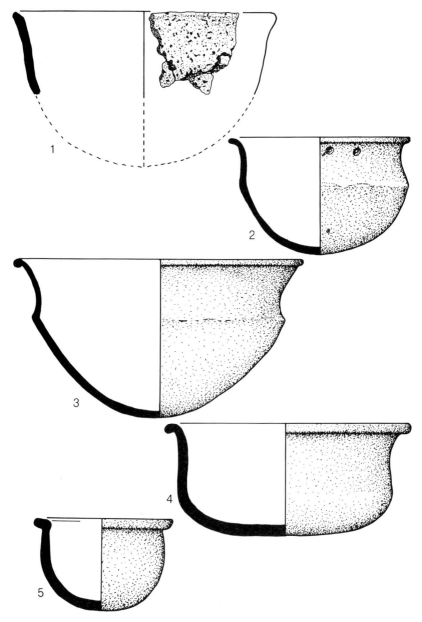

Fig. 2. Grimston ware. 1-2, Thirlings, Northumberland, after Hurrel. 3, Hanging Grimston, North Yorkshire, after Piggott. 4, Heslerton Ware from Heslerton, North Yorkshire, after Piggott. 5, Towthorpe Bowl from Towthorpe, Humberside, after Piggott. All are to a scale of 1:4.

Plate 1. Early neolithic pottery from south-west England. (a) Bag-shaped Windmill Hill pot with lugs, height 172 millimetres (6¾ inches). (b) Open bowl of Hembury ware with expanded 'trumpet' lugs, height 109 millimetres (4¼ inches). Both from Hembury, Devon. (Rougemont House Museum, Exeter.)

Undecorated round-based bowls in the south and west of England can also be divided into local styles, the best known of which is probably the *Hembury* style, which dates from about 3300 bc to around the middle of the third millennium (**3**; plate 1b). The fine vessels of this style were made from the gabbroic clay of the Lizard peninsula in Cornwall, possibly by professional potters, and were traded in large quantities as far as Wessex and beyond. Coarser vessels of this style are usually locally made imitations of the finer vessels, though some of the imitated pottery may also have been made elsewhere than the find site.

Hembury style is also characterised by horizontally perforated lugs (**3**, **1**) which often have expanded ends and are so-called 'trumpet' lugs. The rim forms are frequently simple (**3**, **1**) or slightly rolled (**3**, **2**) and the vessel forms are either simple or open bowls or, more rarely, carinated bowls which have a rather upright neck (**3**, **2**) compared to the concave necks of the carinated Grimston ware.

A second undecorated bowl form in the south and west of England is *Windmill Hill* ware named after the neolithic causewayed enclosure in Wiltshire and which dates from the early

Fig. 3. Hembury Ware from Carn Brea, Cornwall, after Mercer. To a scale of 1:4.

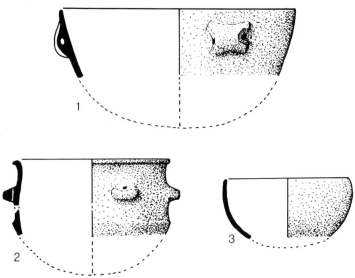

Fig. 4. Windmill Hill pottery from the causewayed enclosure at Windmill Hill, Wiltshire, after Smith. To a scale of 1:5.

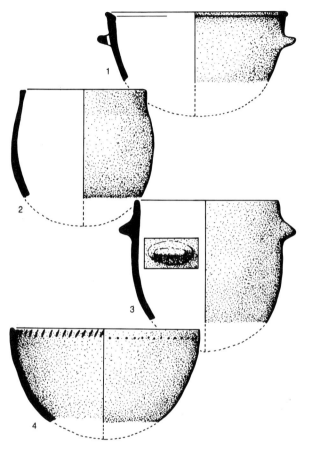

to the middle of the third millennium bc. Windmill Hill pottery tends towards baggy profiles (**4**, 2, 3; plate 1a) with simple rounded rims (**4**, 3, 4). Occasionally the rims may be thickened (**4**, 1, 2) and small oval or circular applied lugs may be found on the exterior of the vessel (**4**, 1, 3). These usually appear in pairs. Decoration is very rare on Windmill Hill ware and appears to be later within the assemblage. If it is found it is simple and consists of small dots or very short incisions placed directly below the rim either externally or internally (**4**, 4).

The appearance of decoration at Windmill Hill coincides with a southern decorated bowl tradition. The decoration employed here is simple and unadventurous comprising small pin-pricks or

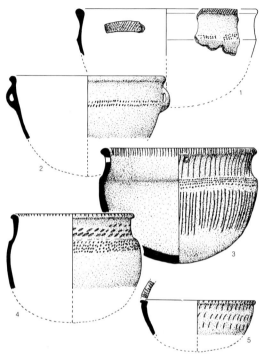

Fig. 5. Abingdon and Mildenhall pottery. 1-2, Abingdon style pottery from the causewayed enclosure at Abingdon, Oxfordshire after Case (1) and Leeds (2). 3-5, Mildenhall style pottery from the settlement site at Hurst Fen, Cambridgeshire, after Clark. All are to a scale of 1:7.

oval to circular stabs, incised lines and, though very rare, twisted cord impressions. There are none of the elaborate and complex impressions of the later neolithic wares. The early neolithic decorated bowls can be seen to have three main regional variations: the *Abingdon* style after the pottery from the causewayed enclosure on the Thames gravels, the *Mildenhall* style after a settlement site in the fens of East Anglia, and the *Whitehawk* style from the causewayed enclosure on Brighton race course in Sussex.

The *Abingdon style* is characterised by bipartite bowls which sometimes have applied lugs or handles on the carination (**5, 1, 2**). These strap handles may be reminiscent of the trumpet lugs of Hembury ware already mentioned. The rims are thickened and often rolled (**5, 1, 2**). They are also frequently decorated with oblique incisions or occasionally twisted cord impressions (**5, 1**). Deep pots and simple bowls are also present in the Abingdon assemblage and these have similar rim forms and decoration to the carinated bowls. Multiple rows of circular stabs or short oblique incisions are the most common decorative elements.

The *Mildenhall* style is rather more elaborately decorated than the Abingdon style and is the eastern English component of the decorated bowl tradition. Once more 'S'-profiled bowls predominate in the assemblage and the pots are often deep with rolled or thickened rims. The rims, necks, shoulders and even the bodies may carry decoration (**5**, 3) though again the motifs and techniques are simple and lack the complexity of later traditions. Rims may be decorated with oblique or transversely parallel incisions or impressions (**5**, 3, 4) whereas the neck decoration tends towards parallel vertical incisions which often extend to the belly of the pot (**5**, 3) and multiple jabs commonly decorate the

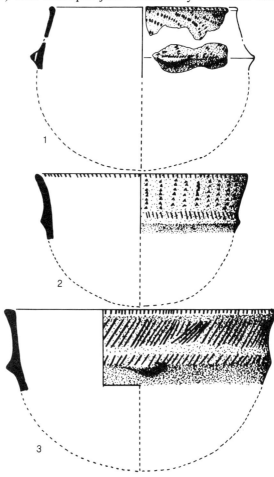

Fig. 6. Whitehawk style pottery from the causewayed enclosure at Whitehawk, East Sussex, after Whittle (1) and Leeds (2-3). 1 to a scale of 1:10; 2 to a scale of 1:5.

shoulder (**5**, 3, 4). These jabs may encroach on to the neck of the pot and may be arranged continuously or metopically. Lugs are rare, but if they are present they are frequently slack and merge with the carination of the pot and they also may be perforated. Internal decoration is also rare but the vertical incisions found on the neck of the pot may find their way into the interior almost as a continuation of the rim decoration.

The third southern decorated bowl style is the *Whitehawk* style. 'S'-profiled, closed and simple bowls are all common in this style as are everted, thickened and simple rims (**6**, 3). Simple oval lugs are common and may also be perforated (**6**, 1, 3). Once more the decoration is unelaborate with the use of simple techniques and motifs in keeping with the other two styles in this series. Stabs and incision are the two main decorative techniques though comb, cord and fingernail impressions are also found. Oblique impressions or incisions decorate the rims (**6**, 1-3), while on the necks parallel oblique or vertical incisions or impressions are most frequently employed (**6**, 2, 3). Occasionally in this area impressions of whipped cord — twisted cord wrapped round itself or some other fine material — may be arranged to form a kind of arcading (**6**, 3). This is the first appearance of whipped cord, which becomes such a popular technique in the later neolithic and earlier bronze age. Oblique incisions or impressions may be used to decorate the shoulders of carinated vessels but decoration rarely extends below this point.

The southern decorated bowl tradition, then, is basically one of simple forms and decoration. The techniques and motifs are primitive and unadventurous though the results may be attractive. Elements such as the appearance of herringbone motif and the employment of twisted and whipped cord techniques herald the richly decorated impressed wares of the later neolithic.

The contexts of the decorated bowl traditions tend to be essentially domestic and ritual. They are found on domestic sites such as the type site of Hurst Fen, Mildenhall, and in the causewayed enclosure ditches of Abingdon and Whitehawk. Their quality and decoration, however, may suggest that they are prestigious pots and may be found in ritual contexts; many causewayed enclosure ditches, for example, show evidence of preferential dumping and ritual activity.

3
Later neolithic impressed wares

From the middle of the third millennium bc there is an increase in the amount of decorated pottery and in the abundance of the decoration. Two main traditions emerge into the archaeological record, impressed ware and grooved ware. The impressed wares were originally labelled *Peterborough* ware after the settlement site which produced large quantities of that pottery. This is now known to be only one facet of a whole range of different styles but as it is so widespread Peterborough ware can be considered first.

Peterborough ware is developed directly out of the round-based bowl forms of the earlier neolithic. It is distinguished by its heavy rim forms, the deep cavetto zone beneath the rims, and the tendency towards increased and elaborate impressed decoration. The bowls are still round-based with the exception of the Fengate style.

In 1956 Dr Isobel Smith divided Peterborough pottery into three main styles, the *Ebbsfleet, Mortlake,* and *Fengate* styles — which were considered to be chronologically and stylistically distinguishable over much of England. Since 1956, however, a great deal more Peterborough pottery has been discovered on excavations and it is now clear that the substyles are only relevant to the south and east of England and that local styles are found elsewhere. It is also now accepted that the Ebbsfleet-Mortlake-Fengate progression is not so clearly distinguished chronologically as was first thought and that there is indeed a great deal of overlap.

It is in the earliest of the styles — the *Ebbsfleet* style — that the closest links with the early neolithic can be seen (7, 1). In this style, the rim is not overaccentuated and the neck is relatively long. The decoration is simple and unambitious, consisting mainly of incisions with some simple impressions (7, 1). Cord impressions are present on this style but are not yet a decorative component. Cross-hatching and herringbone are the most popular motifs.

With the *Mortlake* style the decoration becomes more elaborate and varied (7, 2). Both twisted and whipped cord impressions are common as are bird bone, stick and fingernail impressions which increase in the decorative repertoire. The main physical characteristic of the Mortlake style is the high waist which constricts the neck to such an extent that it becomes

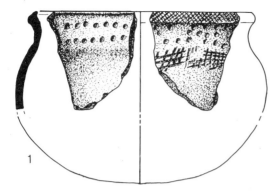

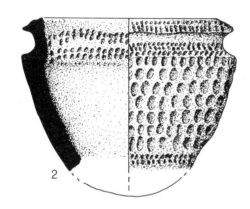

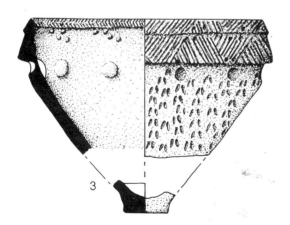

Fig. 7. Peterborough ware. 1, Ebbsfleet style from the settlement site at Ebbsfleet, Kent. 2, Mortlake style from the West Kennet long barrow, Wiltshire. 3, Fengate style from the West Kennet long barrow, Wiltshire. All after Piggott. 1 to a scale of 1:3; 2 and 3 to a scale of 1:4.

a mere cavetto zone beneath the rim. The rim is also much heavier and becomes a platform for the decoration. The flat top of the rim gradually slopes downwards and outwards to form a proto-collar. The bowls are still round-based.

The *Fengate* style continues the rim development of the Mortlake style so that it becomes a heavy collar (7, 3). The neck almost disappears and becomes a slight cavetto zone beneath the collar. One of the most important features is that the body now attains a truncated profile and ends in a flat base. It is this flat base that is a great innovation in the development of the decorated bowl tradition of the neolithic and must be regarded as the result of external influences either from the northern variants of the tradition or from beakers and grooved ware in contemporary use. The base, however, is frequently tiny in relation to the rim diameter and the height of the pot and would clearly be unsteady on even a flat surface. It is therefore unlikely that the base was intended to be functional though the reason for its presence at all is unknown. It is likely that the pot would be kept upright either by suspension or by placing it in a small hole in the ground.

The form of the Fengate style is an exact prototype for the tripartite collared urn of the earlier bronze age. The varied decorated techniques of the Mortlake style continue in use, but their arrangement is rather constricted. Fingernail impressions become more common and incised decoration takes over from the impressed techniques in the filling of the collar (7, 3).

The dating of the three styles is difficult and can only be given in general terms (see chronological chart on page 6). It is clear that there is a stylistic progression and development from the Ebbsfleet style through to the Fengate style, but it must also be remembered that there was probably a period when all three styles were in contemporary use. As a broad general rule, however, it may be said that the Ebbsfleet style made an appearance at the beginning of the second half of the third millennium bc, that the Mortlake style appeared towards the end of the millennium and that the Fengate style appeared towards the beginning of the second millennium, around 1850 bc.

As has been stated, this development is only relevant to the south and southeast and in the north there are regional styles and variants that do not conform to the Ebbsfleet-Mortlake-Fengate progression. More work is needed on these northern wares but as yet it is safer to place local styles such as *Meldon Bridge, Ford,* and *Rudston* within a northern Peterborough tradition as it is with

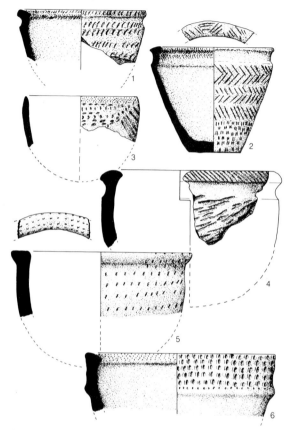

Fig. 8. Northern impressed pottery. 1, Meldon Bridge style from the settlement site at Meldon Bridge, Borders, after Burgess. 2, Rudston style from Rudston, Humberside, after Manby. 3, Scottish impressed bowl from Glenluce, Dumfries and Galloway, after McInnes. 4, Ford style from Ford, Northumberland, after Longworth. 5, Scottish impressed bowl from Glenluce, Dumfries and Galloway, after McInnes. 6, Scottish impressed ware from Brackmont Mill, Fife, after Longworth. 1 and 2 to a scale of 1:9; 3-6 to a scale of 1:6.

that tradition, and particularly the Mortlake style, that the northern vessels have the greatest similarity.

The *Meldon Bridge* style of the Borders and southern Scotland is similar to the Mortlake style but is characterised by the more angular rim forms with internal bevels and external mouldings (**8**, 1) and they thus resemble more the rim forms of the later food vessels than their southern Peterborough counterparts. A variety of impressed and incised decoration is employed with twisted cord and bird bone impressions being the most common. The motifs are generally simple, herringbone predominating, but they cover the whole of the exterior and the rim of the vessel. No bases survive from the Meldon Bridge style (**8**, 1) but the trunconic form of the belly may be indicative of flat bases on at least some of the vessels.

The *Rudston* style of Yorkshire is again related to the Mortlake style of the south but it is characterised by its 'T'-sectioned rim (**3**, 2) which may owe its development to Towthorpe bowls. Incised and impressed techniques are again found in simple motifs but cover the rims and exterior of the pots. In the Rudston style flat bases are common and again the forms of the vessel would resemble as much the later food vessels as Peterborough ware *sensu stricto*.

In Northumberland the *Ford* style links the Meldon Bridge and Rudston styles. The Ford style is named after sherds from the north of the county which have large round-topped rims which are elaborately decorated (**8**, 4). The style is again related to the Mortlake pottery of the south with its deep cavetto zone beneath the rim and its all over impressed or incised decoration. Cord impressions are the most commonly employed decorative technique.

The later neolithic impressed wares of Scotland deserve much future research. It is clear that regional styles here wait to be recognised amidst a mass of sherd material. Later neolithic pottery from Glenluce on the west coast and Brackmont Mill on the east coast exhibit round-based bowl forms with bird bone, whipped cord and fingernail impressions in keeping with the southern material (**8**, 3, 5, 6). The Mortlake forms have disappeared, however, and it may be wrong to equate these Scottish vessels with the Peterborough tradition *sensu stricto*. For this reason the blanket term of *Scottish impressed wares* must be employed until a better alternative is provided.

Later neolithic impressed pottery is found generally on domestic sites in pits and in midden material. Many of these sites lie in river valleys or in open areas and this situation coupled with the presence of bird bones on the vessels may suggest that wild fowling was an important element in the economy of the society. Only rarely is impressed ware found in sepulchral contexts though it is found in the blocking material of the West Kennet chambered long barrow in Wiltshire and with inhumations at Church Dale in Derbyshire.

4
Grooved ware

The second major potting tradition of the later neolithic in Britain is *grooved ware*. This was first defined by Piggott in 1936 primarily from material discovered on coastal sites in Essex. The pottery is clearly distinguished from Peterborough ware by the overwhelming use of grooved, incised and cordoned decoration and by the appearance of tub- and bucket-shaped vessels with flat bases. This type of pottery was also noted at the ritual monument of Woodhenge in Wiltshire and at the neolithic villages of Skara Brae and Rinyo in the Orkney Islands. In 1954 Piggott drew attention to the similarities between the English and the Orcadian material and suggested that the material be called *Rinyo-Clacton* ware to emphasise the geographical extent of the pottery's distribution.

Two years later, in 1956, Isobel Smith divided Rinyo-Clacton ware into four styles, *Rinyo, Clacton, Woodhenge* and *Woodlands,* but at that time the quantity of pottery involved was still quite small.

In 1971 a large corpus of pottery was compiled by Longworth, who advocated a return to the name grooved ware in preference to Rinyo-Clacton. Longworth also succeeded in identifying four styles, the same as Smith's but substituting the name *Durrington* style for the Woodhenge style. It is still debated whether to use the term Rinyo-Clacton or grooved ware and both terms appear in the archaeological literature referring to the same ceramic. As grooved ware best describes the physical characteristics of the pottery, which is the main concern of this book, the term is favoured here.

The *Clacton* style of grooved ware is defined by four main characteristics (**9**, 1). The rim is often simple and rounded with either grooved decoration or plastic decoration on the interior of the rim. The exterior of the pottery is frequently decorated with incised or grooved triangles, lozenges, or rectangles. These are usually filled with stabbed ovals or circles (**9**, 1). Multiple incised running or opposed chevrons are also frequently found on the exterior of the vessels. It must be emphasised that not all of the vessels in the Clacton style need bear all of these traits but simply that these traits are the most frequently occurring and one or all may occur on each vessel. The Clacton style is named after the settlement complex on the submerged land surface found on the

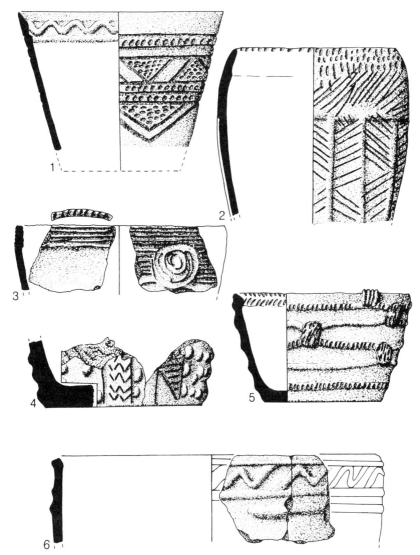

Fig. 9. Grooved ware. 1, Clacton style from Clacton, Essex, after Longworth. 2-3, Durrington style from Durrington Walls, Wiltshire, after Longworth. 4, Grooved ware from Skara Brae, Orkney, after Childe. 5, Woodlands style from Woodlands, Wiltshire, after Stone. 6, Grooved ware from Skara Brae, Orkney, after Fraser. 1-3 to a scale of 1:6; 4 and 6 to a scale of 1:3; 5 to a scale of 1:2.

Essex coast where grooved ware and beaker sherds were common.

The *Durrington* style is named after the large Wessex henge monument of Durrington Walls in Wiltshire. The style is distinguished by six main characteristics: the rim is frequently internally bevelled, the bevel is often concave (**9**, 2) and carries incised decoration; grooved spirals or concentric circles are used to decorate the exterior (**9**, 3); vertical cordons often divide the exterior into strips or panels (**9**, 2). The last three characteristics are the uses of multiple incised lines and filled triangles to decorate the exterior, and the use of twisted and whipped cord impressions, which link the pottery to the Peterborough tradition albeit in a very minor way. The form of the Durrington vessels is usually that of a deep bucket-shaped pot often with an inturned rim (**9**, 2).

The *Woodlands* style is named after the pottery from a number of ostensibly domestic pits. The style is characterised by small squat vessels (**9**, 5) carrying horizontal and converging applied and raised cordons which may be either plain or decorated with short incised lines. Applied pellets of clay often 'knot' the cordons together. Ladder patterns may be found on the exterior of the vessels and on the interior of the rims. Perhaps the most distinctive characteristic of the Woodlands style after the applied cordons is the applied pellets of clay that appear on the top of the rim (**9**, 5). These are presumably decorative as they seem to perform no practical function.

Largely confined to the north of Scotland but also with examples in Yorkshire is the *Rinyo* style named after the pottery from the neolithic village of Rinyo in the Orkney Islands. This is characterised by scalloped rims and internally stepped rim bevels. The exterior is frequently decorated with applied pellets (**9**, 4) or roundels and with geometrically arranged cordons (**9**, 6), impressed dot decoration or parallel grooves.

Though these subdivisions of grooved ware are based on decorative techniques and motifs, the styles show no real regional or chronological cohesion, with the possible exception of the Rinyo style. The archaeological contexts from which grooved ware has been retrieved also show considerable variation across the ritual/domestic spectrum. The type sites of both Rinyo and Clacton are domestic sites whereas Durrington Walls is a ritual monument. The presence of grooved ware in sepulchral contexts is less common though it has been found in the blocking of the chambered long barrow at West Kennet and in the filling of the chambers of the passage grave of Quanterness in the Orkney Islands.

While Peterborough ware can be traced to the early neolithic decorated bowl tradition, the origins of grooved ware are more obscure. It may be possible that it originates in Scotland where the earliest dates for grooved ware are found, those from Skara Brae indicating about 2500 bc. In southern Britain, grooved ware was established by about 2000 bc. The applied cordons, particularly on the Woodlands and Durrington styles and the infilling incision common on all the styles has led people to suggest basketry techniques for the origins of grooved ware but this is difficult to prove. The decorative motifs are, however, paralleled in other media in late neolithic Britain and in particular in the rock art of the Irish passage graves and of the north of Britain. This decoration and the presence in Ireland of plain and ridged bucket-shaped, flat-based pots may possibly suggest an Irish origin and the fusion of ceramic and art forms. This is reinforced by the recent discovery of Clacton grooved ware in Ireland and the presence in Britain of undecorated and ridged grooved ware, like the Lough Gur Class II pottery of Ireland. Though the exact relationship between the megalithic art and the decorative motifs of grooved ware are difficult to pinpoint, the parallels are too numerous to be meaningless.

The vessel forms are similarly difficult to find ancestors for and in particular the flat bases which are certainly functional unlike those of Fengate ware. Presumably the shape of the vessels is directly related to their function and the needs of their users. It would suggest that they had flat surfaces as on uneven surfaces round-based pots are far more practical. Because of the association of grooved ware with ritual sites contemporary with the megalithic period and the floruit of astro-archaeology, Mackie has suggested that grooved ware should be regarded as the special pottery of an elite priesthood. His theory of astronomer priests has not, however, received universal acceptance.

5
Regional neolithic forms in Scotland

In the north and west of Scotland the pottery forms become much more regional and resemble more closely contemporary pottery in Ireland than the southern British material. The vessels are still round-based and are decorated with incisions and impressions. In the Clyde area two main styles prevail in addition to the Peterborough related areas already mentioned. These are the *Rothesay* and *Beacharra* styles (**10**, 3 and 5). The *Rothesay* style is recognised by its baggy profile and with its maximum diameter occurring at the rim (**10**, 3). Lugs are another common feature on this style of pottery and they are normally applied and number two or four. The rims are externally simple but internally bevelled and this bevel is often a platform for simple decoration, rarely more than oblique incision.

Vessels in the *Beacharra* style are basically bipartite round-based bowls with the maximum diameter occurring at the carination (**10**, 5). The necks are concave and lead to simple rounded rims. Despite the slightly everted rims, the rim diameter is frequently considerably less than the maximum. Beacharra pots are decorated in the main with incised lines on the neck and on the belly. Parallel lines or arcading are the most frequently used motifs (**10**, 1, 5, 7.)

In the west of Scotland and the Hebrides the carinated bowls persist but become more elaborate and form a distinctive ridged *Hebridean* bowl (**10**, 2). These are deep baggy vessels with multiple carinations and cavetto zones. They are round-bottomed and have their maximum diameters about midway up the total height of the vessels. The rim forms are normally flat-topped and thickened. The decoration is simple and usually consists of obliquely incised lines which change direction from cavetto zone to cavetto zone to produce an interrupted herringbone motif (**10**, 2).

Fig. 10. Scottish regional neolithic bowls. 1 and 7, Unival neolithic cairns, after Scott. 2 and 6, Northton, Isle of Harris, after Simpson. 3, Rothesay style from the type site, after Scott. 4, Rudh' an Dunain, Isle of Skye, after McInnes. 5, Beacharra bowl from the neolithic cairn at Beacharra, after Scott. 8, Unstan bowl from the neolithic cairn at Unstan, Orkney, after Henshall. 1, 2 and 4-7 to a scale of 1:3; 3 and 8 to a scale of 1:4.

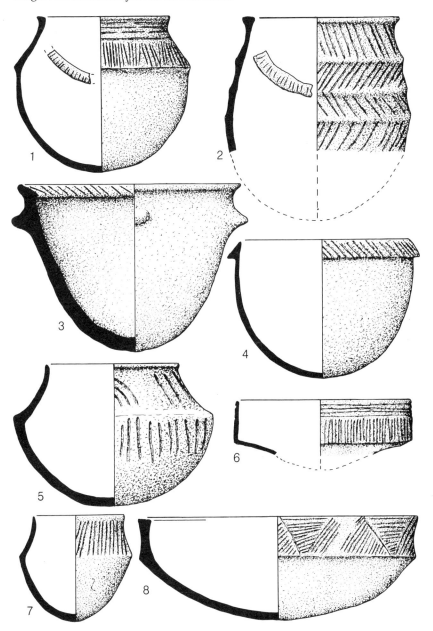

Finally, in the north and west of Scotland is found the *Unstan* bowl named after the pottery found in the megalithic stalled cairn in Orkney. This varies in form but consists essentially of a straight-sided bowl superimposed on a round base to form a bipartite, almost collared vessel (**10**, 6, 8). The angle between the neck and the round belly is often so accentuated as to produce the impression of a collar. The rim forms are simple and the decoration is usually incised, though stab and drag techniques are also employed from time to time. The decoration is usually confined to the upper part of the vessel and consists mainly of parallel lines. These are often arranged either vertically or horizontally (**10**, 6) or are grouped into filled triangles (**10**, 8).

In the neolithic stone houses of the Shetland Isles in the far north, the pottery becomes predictably more idiosyncratic. Flat-based 'S'-profiled pots are present and are decorated almost entirely by incisions grouped into crude and haphazard geometrical designs, and in particular vertical herringbone. These vessels are frequently decorated on the neck and on the body and have an undecorated waist. As such they resemble, albeit vaguely, necked beakers and it is more than probable that they represent a local attempt at beaker imitation.

6
Beakers

While in previous chapters the emphasis has been on the indigenous development of the pottery, beakers — or to be precise bell beakers — are an intrusive form of pottery that reached Britain from Europe at the end of the neolithic and start of the early bronze age at the beginning of the second millennium bc. Many attempts have been made to classify beaker pottery but none of them has found universal acceptance and none of them is entirely satisfactory. For this reason, no strict typology will be given here and instead early, middle and late types are illustrated and a basic outline of development is sketched.

The early style beakers reach Britain as fine, well made vessels with sinuous 'S'-shaped profiles and in a good red fabric. The belly of the pot is quite low down (11, 4) and the rims are inevitably everted and simple. There are none of the thickenings or rim mouldings of the indigenous ceramics. Two basic forms of early beakers are found in Britain and are recognised by their decoration. The first is the *all-over cord* or *all-over combed* (AOC) beakers, entirely decorated with encircling lines of twisted cord decoration or toothed comb impressions (11, 1). Occasionally a slight undecorated band may be left immediately below the rim on the outside of the pot and similarly the decoration may extend over the rim into the inside of the vessel. The second type is the *comb-zoned* vessel which, as the name suggests, has narrow bands of geometric decoration executed with a toothed comb and arranged into bands separated from each other by undecorated zones (11, 2). These decorated bands are narrow and filled with uncomplicated designs such as herringbone or cross-hatching.

Middle style beakers exhibit a more adventurous decorative scheme though the technique used is still the same. In essence the decorated zones become broader and their filling more elaborate (11, 3, 4). The shape of the vessel also alters (plate 2a) with more emphasis being placed on the differentiation between the neck and the belly of the vessel (11, 5, 6). The belly of the pot moves slightly higher up the body and the neck of the pot and neck accentuation begins. The zones are fewer in number than on the early style pots. They are also broader and filled with a variety of filled and open geometric patterns. Sometimes the use of comb may be replaced by incision. Also in the middle period, we see

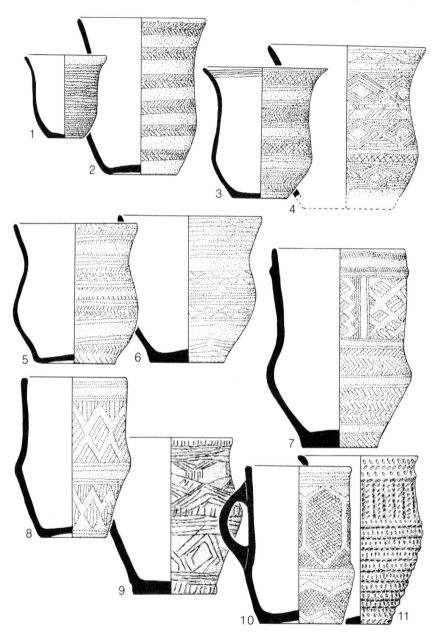

the start of fingernail-decorated beakers. These finger-rusticated pots can be either fine or coarse, the impressions can be arranged randomly or geometrically and the size range of these vessels can also vary considerably. They are most commonly found in domestic assemblages.

Late style beakers represent the floruit and decline of this class of pottery. The neck of the vessel is now accentuated and elongated and the body tends to become rather bulbous (**11**, 7, 8). The decoration has contracted into two main zones (plate 2b), one on the belly and the other on the neck. These zones are filled with a variety of geometric motifs executed in comb or in incision. There is also vertical decoration set within these broad zones (**11**, 7). Very frequently in the late phase there may be a lack of care taken over the execution of some of the incised decoration (**11**, 9). Fingernail-decorated pottery increases both in frequency and size. Pots frequently attain large sizes (**11**, 11) and may have

Fig. 11. (opposite) Beaker pottery. 1-2 Early style beakers. 3-4, Early-middle style. 5-6, Middle style. 7-9, Late style. 10, Late handled beaker. 11, Finger rusticated 'potbeaker'. 1, Cassington, Oxfordshire, after Case. 2, Christchurch, Dorset, after Piggott. 3, West Kennet, Wiltshire, after Piggott. 4, Thickthorn Down, Dorset, after Clarke. 5, Ashton, Northamptonshire. 6, Stoneywood, Grampian. 7, Mouse Low, Derbyshire, after Vine. 8, Brigmerston, Wiltshire, after Clarke. 9, Lilburn Hill, Northumberland, after Tait. 10, March, Cambridgeshire, after Clarke. 11, Somersham, Cambridgeshire, after Clarke. 1-10 to a scale of 1:4; 11 to a scale of 1:6.

Plate 2. Beaker pottery. (a) Middle phase beaker from Newlands, Grampian, height 178 millimetres (7 inches). (b) Late phase beaker from Crawford, Strathclyde, height 127 millimetres (5 inches). (Royal Museums of Scotland, Edinburgh.)

a

b

ribbed and cordoned decoration. These large vessels are frequently called 'potbeakers' after their Dutch counterparts. Handled beakers also make their appearance in the late phase. These may be simply long-necked beakers with handles attached (**11**, 10) or may be smaller tub-shaped handled pots resembling beer tankards. These handled beakers are frequently highly decorated.

At the end of the beaker period there is a total breakdown in the form and decoration. The profile of the pottery slackens considerably, there is an increase in the amount of haphazardly incised decoration and combed decoration declines. Large, open and careless motifs may be used to fill the broad zones (**11**, 9). Beakers then disappear from the archaeological record around 1500 bc almost as mysteriously as they arrived, leaving only phantom traces of zoned and combed decoration in the later indigenous ceramics.

As with the Peterborough styles, there is no firm break between early, middle and late beakers but a great deal of overlap and doubtless there was a period when all three styles co-existed. As a rough guide, however, it may be said that the early styles reached Britain shortly after about 2000 bc while middle style beakers emerged shortly afterwards, about 1900-1850 bc. Late style beakers were certainly being made by 1700 bc and were declining by 1600 bc.

Function is difficult to determine for these pots. Their form, particularly in the case of the late handled varieties, led to their descriptive name of 'drinking cup' in the nineteenth century and has been retained as beaker after the German *'Becher'*. Their appearance on domestic sites as a full range of domestic pottery suggests that they were not solely drinking vessels. Indeed the large flaring necks of the middle and late vessels do not lend themselves to easy drinking. Impracticality alone, however, does not rule out this purpose — consider the Greek two-handled cups or the yard of ale for instance. The finding at Broomend of Crichie in Aberdeen of a horn ladle in association with a beaker may suggest that the contents of the pot might have been thick — broth or honey for example.

As well as on domestic sites, beakers are commonly found in graves. They are usually with single inhumations or cremations and may be associated with other artefacts such as copper alloy knives and archers' wristguards. For the first time we see an emphasis on the individual buried alone instead of communally and with grave goods that may represent personal belongings.

7
Food vessels and food vessel urns

As we have seen, the fineness of beakers and their handled variants led to their alternative if antiquated name of drinking cup. In contrast, the rather heavier and squatter vessels whose solid moulded rims made them unsuitable for drinking were labelled *food vessels*. These are directly related to the Peterborough and Meldon Bridge styles of impressed ware as they have distinct formal and decorative similarities with preference for cord and impressed techniques. Food vessels have flat bases, as do all bronze age pot forms, but retain the heavy rim and cavetto zone of the Mortlake and, in particular, the Meldon Bridge styles.

Food vessels range from 100 to 200 millimetres (4 to 8 inches) high, they have a predominantly, but not exclusively, highland distribution and they exhibit a marked thinning out of distribution south and east of the Severn-Wash line. The density of the decoration also decreases markedly towards the south.

As with beakers, no strict classification of food vessels has been universally accepted though a variety of regional forms have been identified. Overall there are two main divisions, between bowl and vase forms, the latter preferred in the south of Britain and the former in the north and west of the country. Decoration in the north frequently covers the whole of the pot while in the south the decoration is confined to the upper part of the vessel and is also much simpler.

Of the vase food vessels, the simplest form is a bipartite vase (plate 3) with moulded rim, cavetto zone and truncated body, in short, a flat-based Mortlake bowl (**12**, 1-3). The decoration may cover the whole vessel or may be restricted to the upper half including the rim and the rim bevel (**13**, 1). Variants of this basic form may be bipartite vessels with a shoulder groove of varying depth (**12**, 4 and 5) which may be broken by stop ridges (**12**, 5). This vessel with shoulder groove and stops is termed a *Yorkshire vase* as it is in the north of England that this type predominates. A second regional type is the *southern bipartite vase,* which is generally distributed south of the Severn-Wash line. It is similar to the simple bipartite forms of the north but tends to be rather more angular and be more simply and sparsely decorated (**13**, 1). The shoulder is often pronounced and may be emphasised by herringbone or oblique incisions and impressions.

Plate 3. Food vessels. (a) Bipartite vase food vessel from Duncra Hill, Lothian, height 130 millimetres (5⅛ inches). (b) Bipartite vase from Dunbeath, Highland, height 127 millimetres (5 inches). (c) Bipartite vase from Yetholm, Borders, height 114 millimetres (4½ inches). (Royal Museums of Scotland, Edinburgh.)

Ridged vases are so-called because of their horizontal raised cordons occurring on the body of the pot (**13**, 2). They divide the body of the vessel into numerous horizontal cavetto zones of a normally uniform depth. The cordons may also be highlighted by simple decoration or just incorporated into the whole decorative scheme.

Bucket-shaped food vessels are perhaps the most widely distributed food vessel type, presumably because of their simple form. As the name suggests, they are plain, globular or flower-pot shaped vessels (**13**, 3) with simple profiles and decoration, and without carinations.

As with vase food vessels, bowl types also exhibit regional variation and differences of form, and there are many 'grey' areas between distinctive types which defy definition. The simplest bowl type is the *globular British bowl* which is simple and has a wide distribution. It is an open, flat-based bowl (**14**, 1) with a

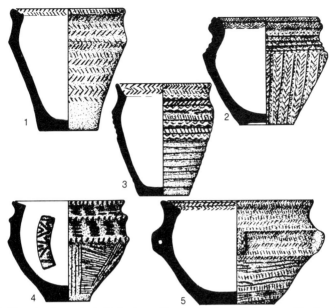

Fig. 12. Vase food vessels. 1, Eglingham, Northumberland. 2, Beanley, Northumberland. 3, Craigbirnoch, Dumfries and Galloway, after Simpson. 4, Haugh Head, Northumberland, after Hurrel. 5, Warkworth, Northumberland. All to a scale of 1:5.

Fig. 13. Vase food vessels. 1, Earl's Farm Down, Wiltshire, after Simpson. 2, Well House Farm, Northumberland, after Hurrel. 3, Castlemartin, Dyfed, after Savory. 1 and 3 to a scale of 1:4; 2 to a scale of 1:3.

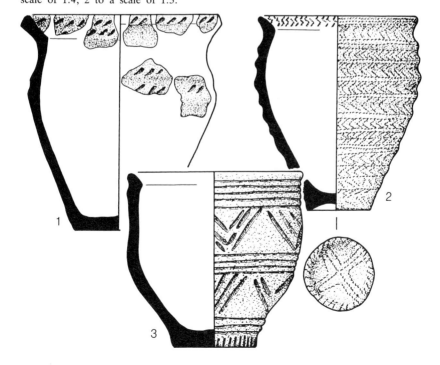

variety of decorative techniques and motifs tending to increase in complexity towards the north and the west (**14**, 2). These features are paralleled in the vase forms. The richly decorated vessels employing false relief and comb decoration are termed *Hiberno-Scottish* bowls after their markedly Scottish and Irish distribution (**14**, 2, 3).

Variations on the basic bowl form can broadly be divided into three main types. Firstly there is the *waisted* bowl (**14**, 5), so-called because of the distinct cavetto zone midway down the pot. This waist may be either decorated or plain and may be emphasised by false relief decoration. An increase in the depth of

Fig. 14. Bowl food vessels. 1, Beanley West Farm, Northumberland. 2, Jesmond, Tyne and Wear, after Hurrel. 3, Corky, County Antrim, after Simpson. 4, Kyloe, Northumberland, after Hurrel. 5, Portpatrick, Dumfries and Galloway, after Simpson. 1-4 to a scale of 1:4; 5 to a scale of 1:3.

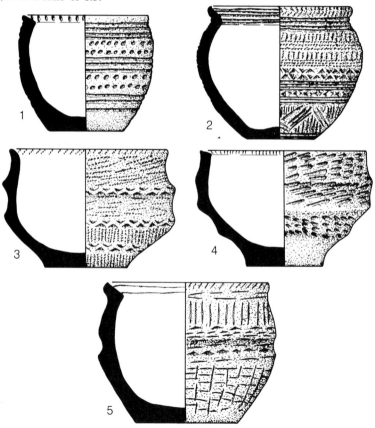

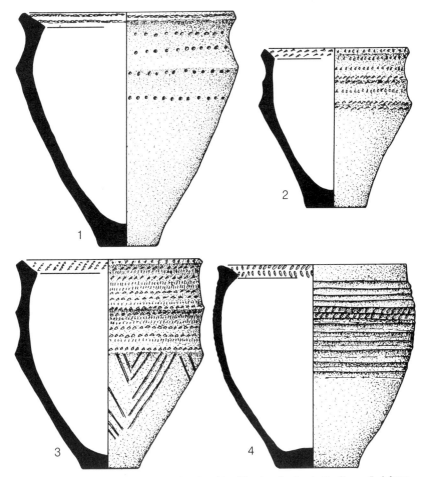

Fig. 15. Enlarged food vessels. 1, Catcherside, Northumberland. 2, Green Leighton, Northumberland. 3, Ferniegair, Strathclyde, after Cowie. 4, Benbeath, Fife, after Cowie. All to a scale of 1:6.

this cavetto zone leads to the tripartite bowl form (**14**, 3) where the bowl is divided into three more or less equal parts. These bowls again have a markedly northern distribution and are thus frequently referred to as *northern tripartite* bowls. Finally, and again paralleling the vase forms, there is the *ridged* bowl whose body profile is broken by multiple horizontal cordons or ridges (**14**, 4). This may be a grooved ware influence on this essentially Peterborough development.

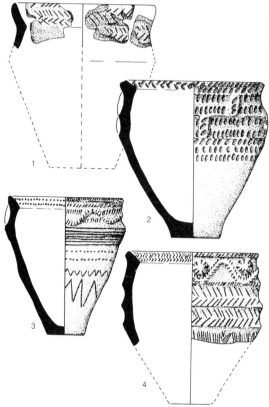

Fig. 16. Enlarged food vessels. 1, Domestic vessel from Kilellan Farm, Islay, after Burgess. 2, Goatscrag, Northumberland, after Hurrel. 3, Ryton, Tyne and Wear. 4, Mid Torrs, Dumfries and Galloway, after Cowie. All to a scale of 1:9.

Food vessels are found in both domestic and funerary contexts. Midden sites in the west of Scotland are producing increasing quantities of pottery of food vessel type and many food vessel forms occur on beaker domestic sites. In graves, food vessels, like beakers, are associated with single burials either by inhumation or cremation. Also like beakers, these burials are found in either flat graves or beneath round barrows.

Enlarged food vessels or food vessel urns

These are simply large versions of food vessels, over 200 millimetres (8 inches) high, which are used to hold cremation burials. It was often generally assumed that food vessels were deliberately enlarged to hold the cremations, but it is now apparent that large forms of food vessel were already in use on domestic sites (**16**, 1). Only vase and bucket forms are enlarged

and exhibit exactly the same characteristics as the smaller vessels.
The decorative techniques and motifs used are the same, twisted
and whipped cord, incision, plastic decoration and stabs, and
their distribution is also markedly northern and western.

Enlarged food vessels are essentially bipartite with or without a
cavetto zone at the shoulder. If this groove is present it may
sometimes contain stops in a manner similar to the Yorkshire
vases (**15**, 1, 2). A variant of this form is found to have multiple
cavetto zones in the neck and all these may contain stops (**16**, 2).
The bucket-shaped enlarged food vessels are a simple form (**15**,
4) with a generally southern distribution. They are usually
sparsely decorated.

A variation on the enlarged food vessel is a type with an
abundance of plastic decoration, often called the *encrusted urn*,
which frequently has applied cordons arranged zigzag fashion in
the neck (**16**, 3, 4), or vertical stops spanning the whole neck, or
else applied roundels and rosettes (**16**, 4; plate 4). It is usually
intricatelly decorated with impressed and applied techniques and
is also extremely pleasing aesthetically. The decoration may
frequently descend below the shoulder of the pot (**16**, 3, 4) but it
is normally in the neck that the most intricate designs occur.
Encrusted urns have been found on domestic sites but are most
commonly found in graves with cremation burials.

8
Collared urns

Like food vessels, *collared urns* are also derived from the later neolithic Peterborough ware and the similarities with the Fengate style are obvious in the heavy collar and truncated body (**17**, 1 and **7**, 3). Like the enlarged food vessels, collared urns are found with cremation burials.

The actual rim forms present on collared urns are numerous, and though simple and flattened rims are found, they are often internally bevelled like food vessels (**17**, 1-6) though they are very rarely externally moulded. The collar may be heavy and strongly emphasised (**17**, 1) or it may be slight and the distinction between the collar and the body little more than a cordon (**17**, 5). In cases such as this, it is often difficult to distinguish between collared and *cordoned* urns.

Collared urns take two basic forms, bipartite and tripartite. The former comprises simply a collar placed on a truncated body (**17**, 1, 2). The tripartite form is however the more numerous type and is recognised by the presence of a cavetto zone beneath the collar (**17**, 3, 4). The depth of the collar and the cavetto zone may vary considerably and occasionally the neck may take up as much as a third of the total vessel height. The total height of collared urns is also variable from less than 200 millimetres (8 inches) in miniature urns to around 500 millimetres (20 inches) and more.

Collared urns retain their Peterborough derived decoration in the form of incision, twisted, whipped and plaited cord, stabs and comb impressions, the latter probably derived from beakers. Herringbone motifs are popular as are filled triangles (**17**, 1, 2, 4), encircling lines (**17**, 3, 4), lattice motifs and metoped decoration or hurdling (**17**, 5). Crescents of twisted cord impressions frequently decorate the shoulder of the pot but decoration rarely descends below this. In bipartite vessels, decoration rarely extends below the collar, but if present it is usually simple (**17**, 2). Incised decoration does tend to become more common in the north and west but it is by no means restricted to these areas and there cannot be said to be a decorative dichotomy. Despite the richness of the techniques and motifs of collared urn decoration not all vessels need to be decorated and undecorated examples are quite common (**17**, 6).

The fabric of collared urns is yet another varying feature and is worthy of mention. The fineness of some urns may rival beaker

Fig. 17. Collared urns. 1, Etal
Moor, Northumberland. 2,
Stonebridge, Northumberland.
3, Brighton, East Sussex, after
Longworth. 4, Cliviger, Lan-
cashire, after Longworth. 5-6
Etal Moor, Northumberland.
All to a scale of 1:9.

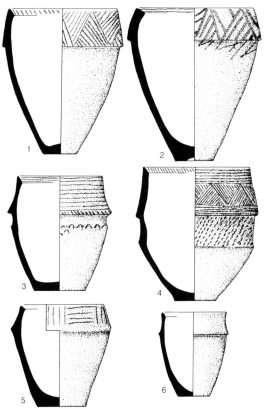

fabrics and may be bright pink, contain finely crushed fillers and
have smooth surfaces. At the other extreme the fabric may be so
coarse and so poorly fired that it is hardly ceramic. The surfaces
may be so poor that often they cannot be retrieved from the
archaeological record by present techniques. Where large coarse
fillers have been added, or where a stony clay has not been
carefully fined, the surfaces may be broken by large stones.

Collared urns are by far the most numerous of the earlier
bronze age urn forms and are the only urns to be found
nationwide from Grampian to the south-west peninsula and from
East Anglia to Ireland.

9
Pygmy cups

The term *pygmy cup* is used to cover a large variety of small accessory vessels usually found in graves and frequently accompanying urns. The name is unsatisfactory as many are clearly not cups in the modern sense as they are too full of holes to have held liquid. The name is now embodied in the archaeological terminology, however, and must be used without prejudice.

Little work has been done on pygmy cups and many regional forms, though doubtless they exist, have not been identified. Nor is their purpose known and indeed it is unlikely that they all served the same purpose. Many could not have held liquid as they either have too many drilled holes (**18**, 1, 3) or have sections cut out of the walls to produce windows (**18**, 2). In some vessels the holes may be for suspension but others clearly have too many perforations just for this (**18**, 3). In earlier literature these vessels are often referred to as *incense cups* as they were thought to have been used for burning incense and this explanation, or the possibility that they were pot-pourri containers, may still be as good as any for the multiple perforated examples.

That 'pygmy cup' is a blanket term is shown by the variety of different vessel forms to which it is applied and which are linked only by their small size. The simplest form is a small pinched bowl with little attempt made to finish it off and no attempt at decoration (**18**, 4). Some finer examples of this type are found on domestic sites as well as in graves. At the other end of the spectrum are fine and intricately fashioned and decorated cups (**18**, 2, 3, 6, 7). There are two main types of these in Wessex, the *Aldbourne cup* and the *grape cup*. The latter type consists of a small cup decorated all over with small applied pellets of clay (**18**, 3, 6) from which they derive their name. The Aldbourne cups are rather different and are in essence bipartite cups with splayed sides in the upper portion and straight sides in the lower half (**18**, 7). The outsides and insides of these vessels are usually elaborately decorated with geometric designs executed in stabbed and incised techniques.

It is difficult to trace a direct ancestry for the pygmy cups. They may have been part of a domestic assemblage later adopted and elaborated for funerary purposes. The applied pellets of the grape cups suggest links with the plastic decoration of grooved ware which may be supported by the geometric decoration of the

Aldbourne cups, though these may equally be beaker influenced. A third possible origin, certainly for the Aldbourne cups, may be the decorated Breton vase support. This is very similar in shape to the Aldbourne cups and frequently has no base but is in effect a ceramic tube with a division midway up the interior forming essentially a pair of opposed and inverted cups. These objects were presumably to support some round-based vessel, probably of wood as round-based ceramics are unknown at this period. It may be said in conclusion, however, that pygmy cups and their individual components of form and decoration are firmly established in the ceramic traditions of the late neolithic but only make their debut in the burial record of the earlier bronze age. They may show some external influences from western France, and are often found with female grave associations.

Fig. 18. Pygmy cups. 1, Wilsford, Wiltshire, after Simpson. 2, Hengistbury Head, Dorset, after Longworth. 3, Wilsford, Wiltshire, after Simpson. 4, Forgan, Fife, after Longworth. 5, Musselburgh, Lothian, after Longworth. 6, Amesbury, Wiltshire, after Simpson. 7, Durrington, Wiltshire, after Simpson. All to a scale of 1:3.

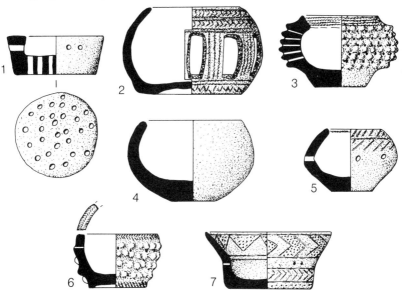

10
Regional urns

The only urn type that is found nationwide is the collared urn but there are a number of other urn forms that have a more restricted local distribution but which are equally important in the richness of the ceramic repertoire of the early bronze age. They all have distinctly regional characteristics.

Handles, for example, are found in the extreme south-west of Britain on *Cornish handled urns* which have an essentially collared urn or *biconical* urn form but which also have strap handles (**19**, 1) adopted from the local *Trevisker* pottery series. The decorative techniques and motifs found on these urns are now familiar and comprise herringbone and lattice decoration in the main with twisted cord and impressed techniques.

The *Trevisker* series itself consists of a wide range of rather flowerpot-shaped vessels and is also restricted to the south-west (**19**, 2-5). The shapes of the Trevisker pots are basically functional and many are found on domestic sites in Devon and Cornwall. Incised decoration is common (**19**, 2-4) but also frequently employed is plaited cord. Herringbone and running chevrons are popular motifs and though shoulder cavetto zones may be present they are usually shallow and almost vestigial. Functional and non-functional lugs are also found.

Biconical urns are also found in the south and south-west and especially in Wessex. Biconical is a term applied to a variety of urn forms but in essence refers to a large urn-shaped pot with a marked carination at the top of a truncated body after which the pot narrows to a rim (**19**, 6). This carination is usually in the upper third of the vessel where a collar would be on a collared urn. The carination may also be emphasised by an applied cordon and if this is the case then it is often difficult to distinguish between collared and biconical urns and the two forms are clearly related. Biconical urns, however, exhibit variety within themselves. The upper portion may, for example, have an everted rim resulting in a concave rather than straight neck (**20**, 1) but the rim diameter is still less than that at the carination. Decoration may consist of cord and comb impressions as well as incision and this is almost entirely restricted to the rim and the area above the shoulder. The shoulder itself may be accentuated by fingernail impressions (**19**, 6). Plastic decoration is also found on biconical

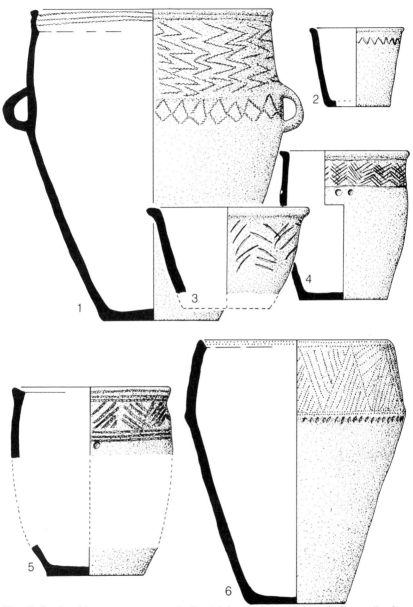

Fig. 19. Regional bronze age pottery. 1, Cornish handled urn, Tregaseal, Cornwall, after Patchett. 2-5, Trevisker pottery from Trevisker Round (2, 4, 5) and Gwithian (3), Cornwall, after ApSimon (Trevisker) and Thomas (Gwithian). 6, Biconical urn from Cherhill, Wiltshire, after Simpson. 3 to a scale of 1:3; others to a scale of 1:6.

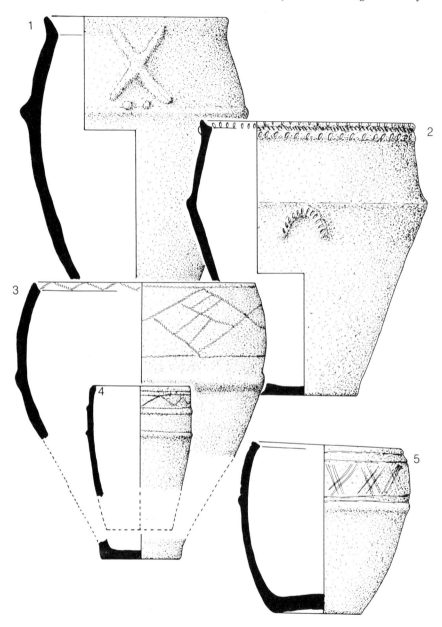

urns but is usually limited (**20**, 1, 2). Horseshoe 'handles', purely non-functional, are commonly found below the shoulder of Wessex biconical urns (**20**, 2).

In northern and western Britain it is *cordoned urns* that predominate (**20**, 3-5). As the name suggests, these urns are characterised by the presence of horizontal applied cordons which divide the body into zones. Two cordons are the most common, one on the upper part of the urn and the other at a varying distance below this (**20**, 4). The positioning of the upper cordon once more resembles the collar of a collared urn and again the two types are clearly related. Urns with a single cordon resemble a bipartite, and those with two cordons a tripartite, collared urn. Cordoned urns with more than two cordons are rare. The basic shape is either barrel (**20**, 3, 5) or bucket (**20**, 4) and the decoration is usually confined to the upper part of the vessel (**20**, 3-5). The decoration also tends to be rather basic using lattice motifs, herringbone and chevrons. It is frequently haphazard and cord and incised techniques are the most used. Simple flattened and internally bevelled rims are common but externally moulded rims are absent.

Fig. 20. Biconical and cordoned urns. 1, Biconical urn from Sturminster Marshall, Dorset, after Calkin. 2, Biconical urn from Bloxworth, Dorset, after Calkin. 3, Cordoned urn from Moralee Farm, Northumberland. 4, Cordoned urn from Limefield, Strathclyde, after MacLaren. 5, Cordoned urn from Thixendale, North Yorkshire, after ApSimon. All to a scale of 1:6.

11
Deverel-Rimbury and the end of the early bronze age

Although originally thought to be later bronze age, radiocarbon dating has shown that the large *bucket, barrel* and *globular* urns of the Deverel-Rimbury tradition are firmly rooted in the early bronze age (see chronological chart). They have their ancestry in the cordoned and bucket-shaped domestic pottery of the late neolithic such as grooved ware or beaker.

The Deverel-Rimbury tradition is named after two burial sites in Dorset and it is entirely a southern English phenomenon. The decoration on all types is rarely complex and consists of cordons, fingertip impressions and grooving.

The name *barrel urn* describes their form. They are large vessels with convex sides and with their maximum diameters occurring about midway up the height of the vessel (**21**, 5). They are decorated with fingernail impressions and cordons, especially vertical cordons running down the height of the vessel. More complex cordons such as zigzags may be found in the upper part of the pot (**21**, 5). The grooved ware ancestry would appear to be evident in vessels of this type. Urns of this class with applied zigzags or with an applied cross on the inside of the base are further set apart and termed *South Lodge urns* after the settlement site which produced a number of them. Rim forms are varied and include a number of expanded and flat-topped types.

Bucket urns also take their names from their basic shape. Instead of the convex sides of the barrel urns they have straight or splayed sides (**21**, 1-3) and are much simpler. Their maximum diameters are usually at the rims (**21**, 1) or just below them (**21**, 2). The rim forms are usually simple or rounded though thickened rims are also present. Cordons and/or lugs may be found on the upper parts of these pots (**21**, 2, 3) and finger impressions are the most common form of decoration.

The *globular urn* is a form that is new to the British early bronze age repertoire and there are two types. In Type I are fine pots with bulbous bodies and constricted necks and rims (**21**, 4). The surfaces are frequently smooth and burnished and the decoration is lightly executed with a blunt point to form horizontal lines and filled triangles, the latter motif usually appearing uppermost in any decorative scheme. Lugs may also

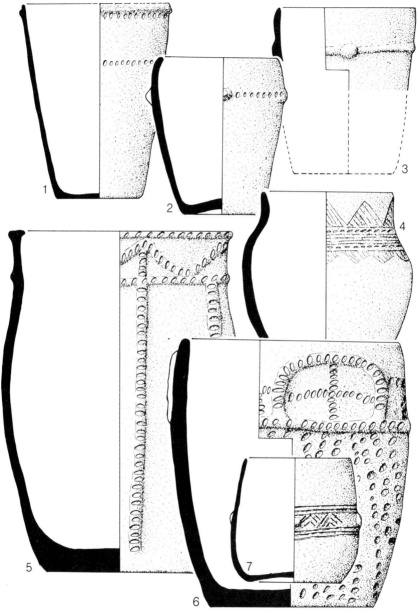

Fig. 21. Deverel-Rimbury pottery. 1, Pokesdown, Dorset, after Calkin. 2, Stourfield, Hampshire, after Calkin. 3, Puddletown Heath, Dorset, after Calkin. 4, Salisbury, Wiltshire, after Langmaid. 5, Bower Chalke, Wiltshire, after Simpson. 6, Ardleigh, Essex, after Burgess. 7, Hillbrow, Hampshire, after Calkin. All to a scale of 1:6.

appear on the shoulders. Type II globular urns, though frequently better fired than class I vessels, often appear rather degenerate (**21**, 7) and have the decoration executed with a sharper point. Another difference is that the uppermost element of the decoration comprises rows of horizontal incision instead of filled triangles. This latter motif is still present, but appears within the motif scheme (**21**, 7).

An East Anglian variant of the Deverel-Rimbury tradition is found in the form of *Ardleigh urns* (**21**, 6) which are recognised by their all-over fingertip impressions as well as the use of

Fig. 22. Regional bronze age urn forms. 1, Cossington, Leicestershire, after Vine. 2-3, Suffield, North Yorkshire, after Manby. 4, Eggleston, County Durham. 5, Green Knowe, Borders, after Jobey. All to a scale of 1:6.

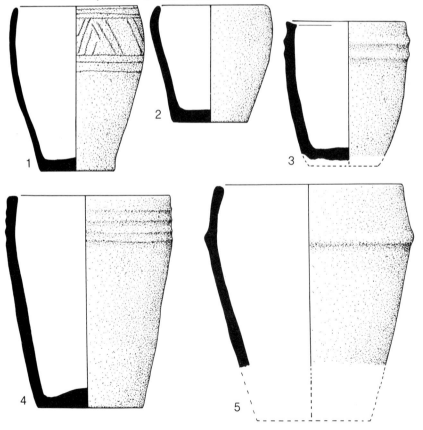

cordons in the decorative scheme. Distinctively regional globular urns are also found in this area.

In the rest of Britain local equivalents, as opposed to local styles, of Deverel-Rimbury pottery are expressed in a variety of barrel- and bucket-shaped urns. In the Midlands, barrel urns are found as are later cordoned urns, and finger and cord impressed decoration is still common (22, 1). The late urns of the Midlands may also be simple undecorated bucket-shaped vessels.

In Yorkshire and the north, late cordoned urns survive but bucket urns and so-called *flat-rimmed* ware are present (22, 2-5). These urns are simple in their profile, frequently undecorated or crudely incised below the rim, and have flat or internally bevelled rims. Some may also be perforated below the rim. A feature of these northern bucket urns may be the presence below the rim of slight grooves, made as if by the potter's fingers running round below the rim to smooth the vessel off (22, 4). These are too shallow to be functional. Flat-rimmed ware is another blanket term used to describe a variety of bucket and barrel urn types and is unsatisfactory as a chronological indicator. Much flat-rimmed, bucket-shaped pottery has been found in neolithic contexts in Scotland.

In the north, late cordoned urns also survive in the domestic and funerary repertoire (22, 5) and thus equate further with the Deverel-Rimbury culture in that the same pot types are being used for both domestic and sepulchral purposes.

12
Glossary

Applied decoration: Decoration which is stuck on to the body of the pot. In the neolithic and bronze age this is usually clay, of the same type as the pot itself, which is stuck on to the wall of the vessel (with water) while the clay is still soft and unfired. It is a technique most commonly used on grooved ware (**9**, 5) and food vessel urns (**16**, 4) and is usually found in cordons, lugs or knobs.

Bevel: The sloping platform on the inside of a rim. It is frequently decorated and is most common on the early bronze age pottery (**16**, 4 and **1**, 12).

Bipartite: Term used to describe a pot which has two basic shapes combined to form the whole. It is most commonly used for early bronze age pottery such as food vessels and urns where the neck or collar forms one element and the truncated body the second (**12**, 2 and **17**, 1). It is used to distinguish from vessels which may also have a *tripartite* form.

Carination: An angle caused by sudden change in direction in the profile of a pot. It may simply form the shoulder of the pot, or there may be multiple carinations. See **1**, 4 and **12**, 2 for instances of single carination and **10**, 2 for multiple carinations.

Cavetto zone: A concave zone encircling the pot and often found between carinations. It may occur immediately below a rim (**8**, 4 and **17**, 3) or at the shoulder, especially of food vessels (**12**, 4). Vessels with multiple carinations will also have as a result multiple cavetto zones (**10**, 2 and **13**, 2). See **1**, 6, 14.

Ceramic: The state that clay achieves when it has been physically and chemically altered by heat. If a pot is properly fired it will be ceramic and resist water, if imperfectly fired then it will not be ceramic and may revert to its clay state.

Coils: In neolithic and bronze age Britain, before the introduction of the potter's wheel, pots were constructed by either pinching out a single ball of clay or by building up and smoothing out rings of clay placed on top of each other. Frequently imperfect bonding can cause a pot to fracture along one of these coils and it will then exhibit a 'coil break'.

Comb: A serrated utensil used to decorate pottery. Archaeological examples that have been found are of bone and have one side notched to form small teeth. These are then impressed into the clay to form a hyphenated line. This form of

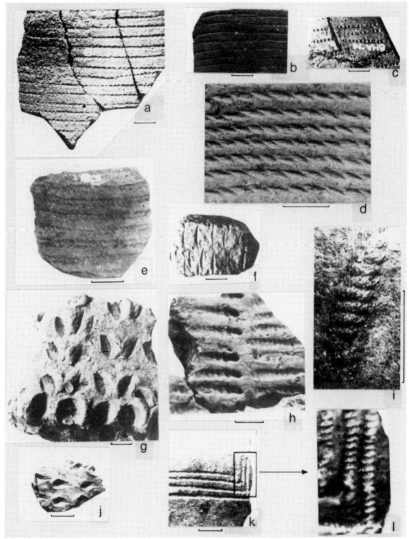

Plate 5. Decorative techniques. (a and b) Square-toothed comb impressions. (c) Round-toothed comb impressions. (d) Twisted cord impressions. (e) Plaited cord impressions. (f) Fingernail decoration. (g) Fingertip impressions. (h and i) Whipped cord maggots. (j) Stab and drag impressions. (k) Whipped impressions using a very fine material. (l) shows a section of k. All scales represent 10 millimetres (⅜ inch).

decoration is frequently used on beakers as well as later
ceramics (**11**, 1-8; plate 5, a-c) and may show either round or
rectangular teeth.

Cord: A wound material such as string or thread used to decorate
pottery. The cord is pressed into the soft clay before the pot is
fired to produce cable impressions. The individual fibres of the
cord can frequently be seen in the impressions (plate 5, d).
Frequently called twisted cord to distinguish it from *whipped
cord* and *plaited cord* (**11**, 1 and **17**, 3; plate 5, d, e).

Decoration: Any non-functional elaboration of the pottery.
Impressed techniques are common in this period as well as
applied decoration. Care must be taken to distinguish between
decorative techniques, that is methods of making the decoration
such as cord and comb, and *decorative motifs*, that is
arrangements of the decoration into panels, herringbone and
so on.

Fillers: These are non-clay materials found in the fabric of the pot
which have been deliberately added to reduce the plasticity of
the clay and to prevent damage to the pot during firing. See
inclusions.

False relief: Decoration formed by the impression of a triangular
point into the wet clay at repeated and regular intervals and
with identical juxtaposed impressions below. This results in a
zigzag of clay standing proud in relief. As the effect is caused
by impressions, it is labelled *false* relief (**14**, 3). It is most
frequently found on Hiberno-Scottish food vessels.

Finger decoration: This is formed by pressing the fingers into the
soft clay of the pottery and is a type of *rustication*. Two main
types of finger decoration are used, *fingertip* decoration where
the whole fingertip is impressed into the clay (plate 5, g) and
fingernail impressions (plate 5, f).

Grog: Pieces of finely crushed pottery added to the clay as a type
of *filler*.

Herringbone: A motif formed by the juxtaposition of oblique
lines sloping in different directions. This may be simple (**12**, 1)
or may be interrupted by either a decorative line (**11**, 2) or by a
carination (**16**, 4).

Incision: Decoration caused by dragging a sharp point across the
still wet clay.

Inclusions: Non-clay materials found in the fabric of the pot.
These can be *naturally occurring* and derived from the local
geology or ecology or can be deliberately added to open the
clay and prevent damage during firing (see *fillers*).

Ladder motif: A decorative motif composed of two parallel lines with perpendicular lines in the space between them resembling a ladder and its rungs. This is very common on beaker ceramics.

Lugs: Pellets of clay, normally juxtaposed, added to the outside of the pot. They take various forms: *simple* (**10**, 3), *perforated*, either horizontally (**12**, 5) or vertically (**6**, 1), or *trumpet*, that is horizontally perforated with expanded ends (**3**, 1).

Maggots: Short impressions of *whipped cord* so-called because of their oval and segmented appearance (**8**, 1; plate 5, h, i).

Metopes: Panels of decoration frequently found on late beakers and which have vertical and horizontal framing (**11**, 7).

Opening agents: See *fillers* and *inclusions*.

Plastic decoration: See *applied decoration*.

Rim moulding: Treatment of the rim to produce an external platform for decoration and to give the rim an angular appearance (**8**, 1; **13**, 1). Plastic decoration may also be added to the interior of the rim to produce internal rim mouldings (**9**, 1, 3 and **1**, 7, 11). See *bevel*.

Rustication: Any treatment to the surface of the pot that has the effect of roughening it. It is commonly used in neolithic and bronze age terms in conjunction with *finger decoration*.

Sherd: Piece of broken pottery, frequently the most common find on an archaeological excavation. Pronounced 'shard'.

Stab and drag: Decoration formed by stabbing a point into the clay and then dragging it along the surface while extracting it (**14**, 4; plate 5, j).

Tripartite: Term used to describe a vessel whose total profile is made up of three distinct sections. Used to distinguish from *bipartite* vessels (**14**, 3 and **17**, 3, 4).

Whipped cord: Twisted cord that has been wrapped round either itself or another material in the manner of a hangman's noose. This is then pressed into the soft clay to produce segmented impressions. See *maggots*. (**16**, 2 and **13**, 3; plate 5, h, i, k, l.)

13
Museums to visit

The following is a short list of museums that have good collections of neolithic and early bronze age pottery. The collections vary in size from the large collections of the British Museum and the Royal and National Museums of Scotland and Wales to smaller displays of local material such as Dundee or Colchester. The displays are, however, important in showing regionally distinctive material as well as more classic pottery types. Intending visitors are advised to find out times of opening before making a special journey.

Aberdeen University Anthropological Museum, Marischal College, Aberdeen AB9 1AS. Telephone: Aberdeen (0224) 4024. Material from the north-east of Scotland; particularly good for beaker pottery.

Alexander Keiller Museum, Avebury, Marlborough, Wiltshire SN8 1RF. Telephone: Avebury (067 23) 250. The important collections from Windmill Hill and Avebury.

Art Gallery and Museum, Church Street, Brighton, East Sussex. Telephone: Brighton (0273) 603005. Contains the pottery from the causewayed camp at Whitehawk.

Art Gallery and Museum, Kelvingrove, Glasgow G3 8AG. Telephone: 041-334 7134. Collection of neolithic and bronze age pottery from south-west Scotland.

Ashmolean Museum, Beaumont Street, Oxford OX1 2PH. Telephone: Oxford (0865) 512651. Important collections from Oxfordshire and the Thames gravels.

British Museum, Great Russell Street, London WC1B 3DG. Telephone: 01-636 1555. Large collection of neolithic and bronze age pottery and in particular the pottery from Greenwell's nineteenth-century barrow excavations in the north of England, and the settlement grooved ware and beaker from the Essex coast.

Castle Museum, Norwich, Norfolk NR1 3JU. Telephone: Norwich (0603) 611277. Important collections of sepulchral and domestic pottery from the Fens and northern East Anglia.

City of Bristol Museum and Art Gallery, Queen's Road, Bristol BS8 1RL. Telephone: Bristol (0272) 299771. Important collection of neolithic and bronze age pottery from the south-west.

Colchester and Essex Museum, The Castle, Colchester CO1 1TJ. Telephone: Colchester (0206) 712490. Has an interesting collection of East Anglian beakers and later pottery.

Doncaster Museum and Art Gallery, Chequer Road, Doncaster DN1 2AE. Telephone: Doncaster (0302) 734287. Contains important pottery of the whole period from the Yorkshire Wolds.

Dorset County Museum, High West Street, Dorchester, Dorset DT1 1XA. Telephone: Dorchester (0305) 62735. Houses a well displayed county collection.

Dundee Museums and Art Galleries, Albert Square, Dundee DD1 1DA. Telephone: Dundee (0382) 27643. Small but representative display of local pottery, particularly beakers and food vessels.

Hunterian Museum, The University of Glasgow, Glasgow G12 8QQ. Telephone: 041-339 8855. Important archaeological collections of the University of Glasgow.

Ipswich Museum, High Street, Ipswich IP1 3QH. Telephone: Ipswich (0473) 213761. Important collections of local pottery, both sepulchral and domestic.

Museum of Antiquities of the University and the Society of Antiquaries of Newcastle upon Tyne, The University, Newcastle upon Tyne NE1 7RU. Telephone: Newcastle upon Tyne (0632) 328511. Important collections from the counties of Durham, Tyne and Wear, and Northumberland. A good display of beakers and food vessels.

Museum of Sussex Archaeology, Barbican House, High Street, Lewes, East Sussex BN7 1YE. Telephone: Brighton (0273) 474379. Houses important material from Sussex.

National Museum of Wales, Cathays Park, Cardiff CF1 3NP. Telephone: Cardiff (0222) 397951. Important collections of the representative neolithic and bronze age pottery from Wales.

Red House Museum, Quay Road, Christchurch, Dorset BH23 1BU. Telephone: Christchurch (0202) 482860. Displays a large collection of pottery and particularly some excellent examples of Deverel-Rimbury ware.

Royal Museums of Scotland, Queen Street, Edinburgh EH2 1JD. Telephone: 031-557 3550. Most important collection of neolithic and bronze age pottery from the whole of Scotland, particularly material from the Western and Northern Isles.

Salisbury and South Wiltshire Museum, The King's House, 65 The Close, Salisbury, Wiltshire SP1 2EN. Telephone: Salisbury (0722) 332151. Complements the Devizes Museum.

Sheffield City Museum, Weston Park, Sheffield S10 2TP. Telephone: Sheffield (0742) 27226. Displays the important material of the Bateman collection excavated in the nineteenth century from barrows in Derbyshire and Yorkshire; large selection of pottery from the whole period.

University Museum of Archaeology and Ethnology, Downing Street, Cambridge CB2 3DZ. Telephone: Cambridge (0223) 359714. Contains a large amount of material from south-eastern England and particularly from around the Fens.

Wiltshire Archaeological and Natural History Society, Devizes Museum, Long Street, Devizes SN10 1NS. Telephone: Devizes (0380) 77369. This is one of the most important museums in Britain for neolithic and bronze age pottery and contains much of the pottery from the Wiltshire barrows and ritual sites, and from around Stonehenge.

Yorkshire Museum, Museum Gardens, York YO1 2DR. Telephone: York (0904) 29745. Important county collections, especially food vessels.

14
Further reading

For ease of reference the bibliography has been broken down into general periods. Where an author deals with more than one period in a single work the reference appears once only in the earlier of the sections. Old references have also been listed. Many of these were written before radiocarbon dating and have since been superseded but they were nevertheless important in their time. Anyone wishing to study the changing thought or history of pottery studies will find them essential whereas the general reader will find them of great interest.

General introductory works
Annable, F. K., and Simpson, D. D. A. *Guide Catalogue to the Neolithic and Bronze Age Collections in Devizes Museum.* Wiltshire Archaeological and Natural History Society, 1964.
Burgess, C. B. *The Age of Stonehenge.* Dent, 1980.
Megaw, J. V. S., and Simpson, D. D. A. *An Introduction to British Prehistory.* Leicester University Press, 1979.

Piggott, S. *Neolithic Cultures of the British Isles.* Cambridge University Press, 1954.
Renfrew, C. (editor). 'The Neolithic' in *British Prehistory: a New Outline.* Duckworth, 1974.

Early neolithic pottery
Calkin, J. B. 'The Bournemouth Area in Neolithic and Early Bronze Age Times', *Proceedings of the Dorset Archaeological and Natural History Society,* volume 73 (1951) 32-70.
Case, H. J. 'The Neolithic Site at Abingdon, Berkshire', *Antiquaries Journal,* volume 36 (1956) 11-30.
Clark, J. G. D. 'Excavations at the Neolithic Site at Hurst Fen, Mildenhall, Suffolk', *Proceedings of the Prehistoric Society,* volume 26 (1960) 202-45.
Clark, J. G. D., and Godwin, H. 'The Neolithic in the Cambridgeshire Fens', *Antiquity,* volume 36 (1962) 10-23.
Curwen, E. C. 'Excavations at Whitehawk Neolithic Camp, Brighton, 1932-3', *Antiquaries Journal,* volume 14 (1934) 99-133.
Henshall, A. S. 'The Neolithic Pottery from Easterton of Roseisle, Moray' in *From the Stone Age to the Forty Five,* edited by A. O'Connor and D. V. Clarke. John Donald, 1983.
Manby, T. G. 'Neolithic Occupation Sites on the Yorkshire Wolds', *Yorkshire Archaeological Journal,* volume 47 (1975) 23-59.
McInnes, I. J. 'The Neolithic and Early Bronze Age Pottery from the Luce Sands, Wigtownshire', *Proceedings of the Society of Antiquaries of Scotland,* volume 97 (1963-4) 40-81.
McInnes, I. J. 'The Sequence of Scottish Neolithic Pottery', *Scottish Archaeological Forum,* volume I (1969) 19-30.
Peacock, D. P. S. 'Neolithic Pottery Production in Cornwall', *Antiquity,* volume 43 (1969) 145-9.
Scott, G. J. 'The Chambered Tomb of Beacharra, Kintyre, Argyll', *Proceedings of the Prehistoric Society,* volume 30 (1964) 134-58.
Smith, I. F. *Windmill Hill and Avebury: Excavations by Alexander Keiller, 1925-39.* Oxford University Press, 1965.
Whittle, A. W. R. *The Earlier Neolithic of Southern England and its Continental Background.* British Archaeological Reports, number S35, Oxford, 1977.

Late neolithic
Burgess, C. B. 'Meldon Bridge: a Neolithic Promontory Complex near Peebles' in *Settlement and Economy in the Late Third and Second Millennia BC,* edited by C. B. Burgess and R. F. Miket. British Archaeological Reports, number 33, Oxford, 1976.
Childe, V. G. *Skara Brae, a Pictish Village in Orkney.* Edinburgh University Press, 1931.
Clarke, D. V. 'Rinyo and the Orcadian Neolithic' in *From the Stone Age to the Forty Five* edited by A. O'Connor and D. V. Clarke. John Donald, 1983.
Longworth, I. H. 'Five Sherds from Ford, Northumberland, and Their Relative Date', *Yorkshire Archaeological Journal,* volume 42 (1969) 258-61.
Longworth, I. H., and others. 'Further Discoveries at Brackmont Mill, Brackmont Farm, and Tent's Muir, Fife', *Proceedings of the Society of Antiquaries of Scotland,* volume 99 (1966-7) 60-92.
Longworth, I. H., and others. 'A Grooved Ware Site at Lion Point, Clacton', *British Museum Quarterly,* volume 35 (1971) 93-124.
Manby, T. G. *Grooved Ware Sites in the North of England.* British

Archaeological Reports, number 9, Oxford, 1974.

Piggott, S., and Burchell, J. P. T. 'Decorated Prehistoric Pottery from the Bed of the Ebbsfleet, Northfleet, Kent', *Antiquaries Journal,* volume 19 (1939) 405-20.

Riley, D. N. 'Neolithic and Bronze Age Pottery from Risby Warren and Other Occupation Sites in North Lincolnshire', *Proceedings of the Prehistoric Society,* volume 23 (1957) 40-56.

Stone, J. F. S. 'Some Grooved Ware Pottery from the Woodhenge Area', *Proceedings of the Prehistoric Society,* volume 15 (1949) 122-7.

Wainwright, G. J., and Longworth, I. H. *Durrington Walls. Report of the Excavations 1966-68,* Society of Antiquaries, London, 1971.

Warren, S. Hazeldine, and others. 'The Archaeology of the Submerged Land Surface of the Essex Coast', *Proceedings of the Prehistoric Society,* volume 2 (1936) 178-210.

Beaker

Abercromby, J. *A Study of the Bronze Age Pottery of Great Britain and Ireland.* Oxford University Press, 1912.

Case, H. J. 'The Beaker Culture in Britain and Ireland' in *Beakers in Britain and Europe,* edited by R. Mercer. British Archaeological Reports, number S26, Oxford, 1977.

Clarke, D. L. *The Beaker Pottery of Great Britain and Ireland.* Cambridge University Press, 1970.

Gibson, A. M. *Beaker Domestic Sites: a Study in the Domestic Pottery of the Late Third and Early Second Millennia BC in the British Isles.* British Archaeological Reports, number 107, Oxford, 1982.

Gibson, A. M. 'Problems of Beaker Domestic Ceramic Assemblages: the North British Material' in *Between and Beyond the Walls: Essays on the Prehistory and History of North Britain in Honour of George Jobey,* edited by R. F. Miket and C. B. Burgess. John Donald, 1984.

Lanting, J. N., and Waals, J. D. van der. 'British Beakers as Seen from the Continent', *Helinium,* volume 12 (1972) 20-46.

Musson, R. C. 'An Illustrated Catalogue of Sussex Beaker and Bronze Age Pottery', *Sussex Archaeological Collections,* volume 42 (1954) 106-11.

Piggott, S. 'Abercromby and After: the Beaker Cultures in Britain Reconsidered' in *Culture and Environment,* edited by Foster and Alcock, 1963, 53-91.

Ritchie, J. N. G., and Shepherd, I. A. G. 'Beaker Pottery and Associated Artefacts in South West Scotland', *Transactions of the Dumfries and Galloway Natural History and Antiquarian Society,* volume 50 (1973) 18-36.

Savory, H. N. 'A Corpus of Welsh Bronze Age Pottery. Part I, Beakers', *Bulletin of the Board of Celtic Studies,* volume 16 (1955) 215-41.

Tait, J. *Beakers from Northumberland.* Oriel Press, 1965.

Early bronze age

ApSimon, A. M. 'Cornish Bronze Age Pottery', *Proceedings of the West Cornwall Field Club,* volume 2 (1953) 36-46.

ApSimon, A. M. 'Food Vessels', *Bulletin of the Institute of Archaeology,* volume I (1959) 24-36.

ApSimon, A. M. 'Biconical Urns outside Wessex' in *Prehistoric Man in Wales and the West,* edited by F. Lynch and C. B. Burgess. Adams and Dart, 1972.

ApSimon, A. M., and Greenfield, E. 'Excavation of Bronze Age and Iron Age Settlements at Trevisker Round, St Eval, Cornwall', *Proceedings of the*

Prehistoric Society, volume 38 (1972) 302-81.

Barrett, J. 'Deverel-Rimbury: Problems of Chronology and Interpretation' in *Settlement and Economy in the Late Third and Second Millennia BC,* edited by C. B. Burgess and R. F. Miket. British Archaeological Reports, number 33, Oxford, 1976.

Barrett, J., and others. 'Characterisation of Deverel-Rimbury Pottery from Cranbourne Chase', *Proceedings of the Prehistoric Society,* volume 44 (1978) 135-43.

Bu'Lock, 'The Bronze Age in the North West', *Transactions of the Lancashire and Cheshire Archaeological Society,* volume 71 (1961) 1-42.

Calkin, J. B. 'The Bournemouth Area in the Middle and Late Bronze Age with the Deverel-Rimbury Problem Reconsidered', *Archaeological Journal,* volume 119 (1962) 1-65.

Clark, M. Kitson 'The Yorkshire Food Vessel', *Archaeological Journal,* volume 94 (1937) 43-63.

Cowie, T. G. *Bronze Age Food Vessel Urns.* British Archaeological Reports, number 55, Oxford, 1978.

Fox, C. 'An Encrusted Urn of the Bronze Age from Wales with Notes on the Origins and Distribution of the Type', *Antiquaries Journal,* volume 7 (1927) 115-33.

Longworth, I. H. 'The Whinny Liggate Perforated Wall Cup and its Affinities', in *From the Stone Age to the Forty Five,* edited by A. O'Connor and D. V. Clarke. John Donald, 1983.

Longworth, I. H. *The Collared Urns of the Bronze Age.* Cambridge University Press, 1984.

Patchett, F. M. 'Cornish Bronze Age Pottery', *Archaeological Journal,* volume 101 (1944) 17-49.

Patchett, F. M. 'Cornish Bronze Age Pottery. Part II', *Archaeological Journal,* volume 107 (1950) 44-65.

Piggott, C. M. 'A Middle Bronze Age Barrow and Deverel-Rimbury Urnfield at Latch Farm, Christchurch, Hampshire', *Proceedings of the Prehistoric Society,* volume 4 (1938) 169-87.

Savory, H. N. 'Welsh Bronze Age Pottery. Part II', *Bulletin of the Board of Celtic Studies,* volume 17 (1957) 196-233.

Savory, H. N. 'A Corpus of Welsh Bronze Age Pottery III', *Bulletin of the Board of Celtic Studies,* volume 18 (1958) 89-118.

Simpson, D. D. A. 'Food Vessels in South West Scotland', *Transactions of the Dumfries and Galloway Natural History and Archaeological Society,* volume 42 (1965) 25-50.

Walker, I. C. 'The Counties of Nairnshire, Moray and Banffshire in the Bronze Age', *Proceedings of the Society of Antiquaries of Scotland,* volume 48 (1964-6).

Index

Page numbers in italic refer to illustrations